Horseshoe Harry
AND THE Whale

Written by
Adèle de Leeuw

Illustrated by
Quentin Blake

PARENTS' MAGAZINE PRESS

NEW YORK

For Cary Bardshaw Hansel
whose forebears helped settle the West.

It was a bright autumn day in Wyoming when Horseshoe Harry's great whaling adventure began. He moseyed on down to the corral to saddle his faithful steed, Pokey. Harry was near seven feet tall, with carrot-colored whiskers and a lopsided grin. His left leg made a perfect arc, and his right leg made another, so that when he stood up straight the two legs together formed the most beautiful horseshoe ever seen—east or west of the Great Divide. That's why he was called Horseshoe Harry.

When Harry was astride Pokey, rounding up cattle or roping stray dogies out on the range, no one noticed. Pokey was a fair-sized horse. Still, Harry's legs dangled so close to the ground that whenever he wanted to 'git along' faster, he simply stretched and ran along with the horse. On six legs instead of four, Harry and Pokey really covered the territory!

But, on this autumn day, Horseshoe Harry just shaded his eyes and looked out across the plains. As far as the eye could see, there was land—land dotted with horses and cows, land with sagebrush and a stray cabin or two.

"Seems to me," Harry sighed, "I've been on this here range for too many years. I'm tired of listenin' to the coyotes howl at night, and I'm sick of seein' land wherever my head turns. I hear tell there's sea water off the coast. And I've a hankerin' to see the sea." There and then, his mind was made up. Harry tossed a few shirts into a big blue bandana, stuck his shootin' irons in his holster—plus one in his left boot for good measure—clapped a broad-brimmed hat on his head and said,

"Git along, Pokey, git along. We're goin' to see the sea." Now Harry had no notion how far Wyoming was from the coast. Fact was, he didn't even know which coast he was headed for, east or west. And he didn't much care.

As it turned out, Harry was traveling due east, and he just kept going for weeks on end. It got colder and colder, and by the time he reached Boston, he was near frozen.

"Which way to the sea, stranger?" Harry asked a passerby.
"Can't you smell it from here?" the man asked, surprised.
"Salt and fish is what I smell. But if that's the sea, I
want to see it with my own two eyes."
"Over that-a-way," the man pointed. "Good luck and don't
fall in."

Horseshoe Harry rode on, and the nearer he came to
the shore, the colder he got. When he saw a brightly
lit tavern, Harry decided to stop in for a hot drink.
He tied Pokey to a hitching post. "I'll be back soon,
ole pal," he said, spreading a warm blanket over the
faithful horse.

It was cozy inside, and Harry ordered a steaming cup
of coffee. Everyone just stared at him—at his
broad-brimmed hat and soft high boots, at his big
blue bandana and shiny shootin' irons.
"Howdy, folks," said Horseshoe Harry.
Several rough-looking men put their heads together.
One walked over to Harry. "You've come a far piece?"
"From Wyoming, pardner," answered Horseshoe Harry.

"I've come to see the sea."

"Well, you'll be seeing it all right," the man said.
His companions guffawed. Horseshoe Harry wondered
what was so funny. "Come over and meet my buddies,"
said his new acquaintance, carrying Harry's coffee
from the counter to a table.

"Sure smells good," said Horseshoe Harry as he lifted
the cup and drank it all down.

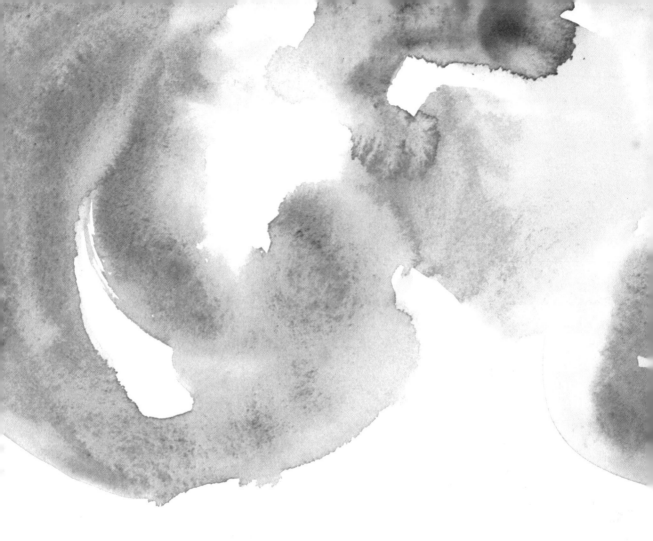

And that was the last Harry knew till he awoke on a hard
floor. When he looked up he saw clouds a-swooping and
a-dipping as they never had in Wyoming.

"I must be on a ship," muttered Horseshoe Harry. "But it
sure weren't any of *my* doin'. Must be those fellas put
somethin' in my coffee, then carted me off." He sat up.
"Now that's more than I aim to take lyin' down. Where's
Pokey?" he yelled, feeling for the shootin' irons in his
holster. Gone!

A big gruff man leaned over him. "I'm the mate.
Who's Pokey?"

"My horse. He'll die of the cold."

"Get up, landlubber," growled
the mate, "or I'll crack your
noggin with this marlin spike."

Horseshoe Harry unfolded himself, near seven feet of him, and he towered over the mate. "That's no way to talk to a gent what asks a civil question. Hand over your weapon!" Harry grabbed the marlin spike and, with one easy motion, flung it into the sea.

"There sure is a lot of water hereabouts," Harry marveled. "Looks like the whole Wyoming plains got flooded."

The mate lunged at Harry but, easy as pie, Horseshoe Harry grabbed him by the collar and held him up in the air. "Now I want this here ship turned around so I can git my horse," he said.

The captain, hearing a ruckus, came down from the
bridge. He was carrying a big bassoon.
"What goes on here?" he shouted.
Quick as a wink, Horseshoe Harry slipped his spare
shootin' iron out of his boot. "You turn this ship
around, Cap'n," he said, "and I'll go easy with you."
"Throw him in the brig!" the captain roared.
Hearing these words, Harry lost his temper.

Taking careful aim, Horseshoe Harry shot off the port side of the captain's great moustache—neat as a pin.

The captain stood still, in shock. Harry aimed again. This time the starboard side of the moustache dropped to the deck.

"Turn this ship around," Harry repeated. Picking up the right and left sides of his moustache with dignity, the captain said, "This ship can't turn around. You're aboard the *Gentle Gertie* and we're headed round Cape Horn."

"I don't aim to stay," said Horseshoe Harry.

"But stay you must," the captain answered.

"We need another sailor. That's why we—ahem—chose you. We're out to catch whales, and we'll be gone two years."

"Two years!" cried Harry. "That's a fearful long time. What about my horse, Pokey? He'll starve."

"Your horse," the captain replied, "is in a warm stable in South Boston. With two years of oats all paid up."

"Well," sighed Harry, "then I reckon I kin take it. I've never seen a whale before—much less catched one."

"By the way," the captain asked, with a gleam in his eye, "how do you like the sound of a bassoon?"

"Horsefeathers! How kin I tell? I never heered one."

"Well, you will," the captain said cheerily. "I play the bassoon. On my ship, there's music—and no back talk."

So Horseshoe Harry resigned himself to a sailor's life. The rest of the crew, who had been on whaling trips before, made fun of him. Harry didn't know an oar from a plank, or a marlin spike from a tent peg. And he thought the harpoon was a giant Apache arrow.

For nigh on a hundred days, the *Gentle Gertie* sailed.
By the time they reached the Indian Ocean, the crew
had seen a hundred or more whales. "Thar she blows!"
the lookout would yell from the crow's nest, "Thar
she blows!"

The men stood by to lower the boats, and the oarsmen
were all at the ready. The harpooners, they were
just itching to do their trick. But that captain,
he just never gave the order to lower away. He was
too busy playing on his bassoon.

"We'll be sailin' this blasted ocean forever," Cranky Chris complained one day. "Whales to port, and whales to starboard. Whales jumpin' out of the sea and sneerin' at us, darin' us to come and get 'em. But the Cap'n, he sits in his cabin, a-playin' that blasted bazzoon."

"I kin hardly stand it myself," Harry said. "Day and night, the same 'oompah, diddle diddle. Oompah, diddle diddle!' It's drivin' me crazy."

" If we catch no whales," Cranky Chris said glumly, "we'll get no oil, and if we get no oil, we'll stow no casks. If ever we get back home to Boston, we'll be poorer than when we left—that's *if* we ever get there."

"I aim to git home," said Harry. "And once I pick up ole Pokey, I'm headin' back to the range."

"Hah!" sneered Cranky Chris. "What can *you* do?"

"Just you wait and see," Harry said. With that, he stood up and stretched, near seven feet of him. Then he marched up to the captain's door. "Cap'n, sir," he said. "I want that there instrument you're a-tootlin' on."

"What for?"

"I'm tired of hearin' you play, sir, and I want to try it myself."

"That's mutiny," said the captain.

"Whatever that is, so be it!" answered Harry. "Now hand over your bazzoon pretty quick, sir." The captain was no match for Horseshoe Harry, who calmly took the instrument and pushed the captain into a corner. Then he went out, locking the cabin door after him.

You could hear that captain hollering all up and
down the deck. "You'll never live to see Boston
again!" said Cranky Chris fearfully.

"No matter," said Harry. "So long as I see Wyoming."
With that, he went to the rail and began blowing
into the big bassoon till his eyes near popped.
The sounds that came out made all the sailors
hold their ears.

But Harry played on and on, till he drowned
out the captain's shouting. He played until
the chords of his neck swelled and his face
turned the color of boiled lobster.

"Sufferin' swordfish!" Cranky Chris yelled. "Look at that. You've gone and charmed a whale."
Sure enough, swimming alongside the ship was

a great whale spouting water. Not only that, it
was doing a regular dance! It rolled and twisted
and cavorted. It disappeared, then came up again,
blowing water like a fountain out of its spout-hole.

All at once, Horseshoe Harry climbed the rail and held the bassoon high. "I knew an old cowpoke's tune would git to you!" he yelled. "That's the kind of playin' we do out on the range. I christen you Sagebrush Sam," he said. And with these words, he flung the bassoon down. It dropped smack into the whale's spout-hole! And a more surprised creature was never seen—not in the Atlantic nor Pacific oceans. As it swam away, the whale must have begun blowing through the bassoon, for, sure enough, it sounded just like the captain's 'oompah, diddle diddle. Oompah, diddle diddle.'

"Well, at least the music isn't here," said Horseshoe Harry with satisfaction. "I'd better let the captain loose."

The captain was so mad he near burst all his buttons. "Where's my bassoon?" he yelled. "Give it here this minute!"

"Can't do that, Cap'n, sir," said Harry respectfully.

"Why not?"

"It—uh—fell overboard and lodged itself in a whale's spout-hole, or whatever you call it."

"Which whale?"

"One out yonder. Fact is, he's playin' for all he's worth, and it sounds a powerful lot like your playin', sir."

The captain rushed to the rail. "Lower away!" he bellowed.
"Catch the whale that has my bassoon. And don't come back
without it!"

What welcome words! They were going whaling at last!

"Lower away!" the mate repeated.

"Lower away!" the crew echoed happily. They piled into the
boats, which were eased into the sea. The helmsmen steered
for the whale cavorting in the far distance, and the
harpooners stood at the ready.

It was a long time before they came back. The captain
peered over the rail. "Got my bassoon?" he shouted.

"No sir, Cap'n, sir. That we haven't. But we got four other
whales. They were cavortin' around this here—ahem—
Sagebrush Sam. We caught 'em easy."

The men were happy. Even the captain couldn't help being
a little happy, because they had caught four whales, which
meant oil for thousands of lamps. And that meant money for
the men of the *Gentle Gertie* when she returned to Boston.
Next morning, bright and early, the captain ordered
the crew out again. "Catch me that music-spoutin'
whale!" he ordered. "AND BRING BACK MY BASSOON!"

They tried. Oh, how they tried—at least they said
they did. But somehow it was easier to catch the
whales listening to Sagebrush Sam's music than to
catch Sagebrush Sam himself. He just went oompah-
diddling off as soon as the crew neared. Before long,
the *Gentle Gertie* was so full of whale oil her seams
were fit to burst.

And the smell of boiling oil that rose from her deck was enough to turn Horseshoe Harry green as prairie grass.

At long last, the *Gentle Gertie* turned and sailed for home.
The men were so happy they danced a hornpipe
every night.

When they pulled into Boston Harbor, and the money
was divided, Harry found a music store and bought the
captain a new bassoon—even bigger than the one he'd
lost at sea.

Next, Horseshoe Harry headed straight for South
Boston to reclaim his faithful steed, Pokey.
What a joyful reunion the old friends had!

Then Horseshoe Harry settled his broad-brimmed hat on his head and stowed his shootin' irons in his holster —plus one in his left boot for good measure. "Git along, ole pal," he said to Pokey. "I've seen the sea, and I must say it's highly overrated. It'll be good to git back home to Wyoming again."
And it was.

Adèle de Leeuw, a lifelong storyteller, acquired much of the raw material for her 74 books from years of worldwide travel. While serving as a librarian in her hometown of Plainfield, New Jersey, she both instituted and organized the library's story hour. Eager to find a tall tale that would also be a read-aloud spellbinder, she decided to write her own. The result is *Horseshoe Harry and the Whale*, her first book for Parents' Magazine Press.

Quentin Blake is increasingly admired for his wry, comic caricatures which appear regularly in English newspapers, magazines and on BBC-TV. He is also the illustrator of several refreshingly original children's books. A Londoner, Mr. Blake is a tutor in illustration at the Royal College of Art. *Horseshoe Harry and the Whale* marks his first appearance on the Parents' Magazine Press list.